Stocks Trading

Make Money Fast & Easy by Trading Stocks Smartly & Efficiently with this Handy Guide

Table of Contents

Introduction

I want to thank you and congratulate you for downloading the book, *"Stocks Trading: Make Money Fast & Easy by Trading Stocks Smartly & Efficiently with this Handy Guide"*.

Trading stocks to make fast and easy money definitely has its appeal. If you are currently on a job, you know that generating income through sitting on your butt from eight in the morning to five in the afternoon is an exhausting and inefficient way to do it. As your salary is based on how many hours you spend working, the problem lies on the fact that you need to live your life and not spend every hour of every day working. However, since you need money, you push yourself to the limit and end up miserable because you have worked for more than forty hours a week and you still do not have enough money for whatever goal you have in mind.

Now, with stocks trading, things are different. The most important benefit it has and the most notable difference it holds over having a traditional job is that it provides you with easy income. You provide the money and your money works hard for you. Furthermore, it is much more beneficial for you if you invest your money in stocks rather than letting it rot in your bank where it only accrues a small amount of interest. If you invest it in the stock market, you give your money more power to earn. And another amazing thing about stocks trading? You do not need to work technically. With this book, you will learn that all you have to do after teaching yourself of the basics about stocks trading is place orders through your broker, wait for the results, and go gardening. If things go right, you will attain easy money without breaking ten buckets of sweat.

Furthermore, stocks trading is not just for the millionaires. Even small-time investors are free to dabble in it. Race, gender, social standing, among other socio-economic factors, do not matter as long as you have the drive and the interest to engage in stocks trading.

But, you need to remember some things though before you begin trading. First, you need to have a capital. You would not have anything to invest with without some capital to work on. In addition, you also need to develop a logical trading system that proves effective for you. Also, be warned that you will be facing figures and numbers so if you are math-phobic, good luck to you.

So, are you ready? Yes? No? Do not worry, though. This book will definitely guide you to making money by trading stocks smartly. With detailed steps on how to go about buying and selling stocks, this handy companion will help you gain a better understanding of stocks and the world of the stock market.

Thanks again for downloading this book, I hope you enjoy it!

Chapter 1   Trading Terms

Before we proceed, there is nothing better than immersing ourselves in a little exercise of word familiarization. In this chapter are several of the words that you are going to encounter when you are trading stocks.

1. Bear Market

    This term refers to a period when the stock market declines generally. Bear markets are a nightmare for investors looking for profitable stocks.

2. Bull market

    Bull market refers to a period when the economy is doing well, the gross domestic product is increasing, and stock prices are rising. In short, things are bubbles and sunshine! Trading stocks during a bull market is very much ideal for you. But, like all good things, they won't last forever and can be risky if stocks end up being overvalued.

3. Capital gain

    This refers to the difference between the price at which you bought an investment and the price at which you sold it.

4. Diversification

   This is a method of reducing risk by trading in a variety of securities.

5. Dividends

   Dividends are the share of the company's after-tax earnings distributed to stockholders.

6. Dollar-cost averaging

   This refers to the method of purchasing on a regular schedule a fixed dollar amount of a specific investment. This is done no matter what the share price is. Whenever prices are high, fewer shares are bought. On the other hand, when prices are low, more shares are bought.

7. Portfolio

   The portfolio is the collection of all of your investments.

8. Return on Investments

   This refers to the money that is being profited from investments over a certain period. If it is for a specific number of years, it can be termed as annualized returns.

9. Risk

   This refers to the chance that you might lose a part of even all of your original investment. Generally, when the potential gain from an investment is great, the risk that you will lose your money is also high.

10. Shareholder's equity

    This is the difference between the company's assets and liabilities.

11. Stocks

    Stocks represent your ownership in a company that issues it.

12. Street name

    This describes any securities kept by your brokerage firm in your name.

13. Volatility

    The degree to which a security, including stocks, varies in value. Generally, the more volatile your stock is, the higher the risk of losing money.

Chapter 2   Getting Started on Stocks Trading

A stock refers to a share of ownership in a specific company that issued it. To have a stock in a company means that you have a claim on a portion of its assets and profits. When you attain more stock, your stake in the company increases.

Owning a stock makes you one of the many owners of the company and entitles you to what the company owns. At the end of the day, you own a share of every contract of the company, every asset, every piece of furniture, etc. For example, let us say that Amazon issues 1,000 stocks and you bought one share of Amazon. This indicates that you own 1/1000 of what Amazon owns. Whatever decision the management of Amazon makes, the approval of you and the other 999 buyers of Amazon's stocks would have to be sought out. Stockholders are actually the ultimate authority in the company since the power of planting directors into the company's board lies in your hands.

Stocks are represented by stock certificates, which are fancy pieces of paper that serve as proofs of your ownership. However, in this age where business processes are ran electronically, stockholders do not physically see stock certificates because brokerage keeps these records. In addition, although stocks give owners certain claims, the good thing about them is that owners would not be under any obligation if ever the company faces any lawsuit and other cases that could be detrimental to it.

In general, there are two kinds of stocks: common stocks and preferred stocks. Common stocks are more widely traded compared to preferred stocks.

Common stocks are what we know of as shares. They symbolizes one's ownership of a part of the company. Whoever owns a share of a company's common stock gets to vote on matters pertaining to it. Having more stocks equals more votes for you. Whenever the value of the company increases, stockowners generate money because the price of the stock went up consequently. This is what we call capital gain.

Preferred stock, on the other hand, differs from common stocks in the sense that whoever owns them get to have the dividend payments before common stock owners can. Dividends refer to the portion of a company's after-tax profit, which is distributed to the stockholders. In addition, when a company goes out of business, those who own preferred stocks get paid first of their share of whatever is left of the company before the same thing happens to owners of common stocks.

However, the reason why preferred stocks are not more widely bought compared to common stocks is how they are not issued until common stocks have been. Most importantly, even though preferred stockowners get to have access to the dividends before common stockowners do, they usually are paid a preset amount dividend regardless of how much the company made.

For individual investors, trading common stocks usually have more appeal compared to preferred stocks.

Stocks are mostly traded on exchanges, which refer to places where buyers and sellers meet to decide on a stock price. Exchanges come in two platforms: physical and electronic. The physical platform is called a trading floor. You have probably seen what it looks like in TV and in movies. Remember scenes with traders waving, throwing their arms up, screaming, and signaling to each other? Yep, that is pretty much what a trading floor looks like and what you will see in stock markets.

Stock markets are avenues wherein the exchange of securities between buyers and sellers is facilitated. Stock markets reduce the risks that come with investing. Stock markets are like farmers' market, albeit sophisticated ones, that connect buyers and sellers so that those who want to sell stocks do not have to go around in communities trying to find buyers.

Chapter 3   Stocks and the Process of Trading It

What exactly does it mean to trade stocks? Trading stocks involve the buying and selling of it. And buying them is not like the traditional purchase of goods in the supermarket wherein you choose your product and line up before a cashier. In fact, you do not even have to go to a physical stock market, flail your arms around, and yell your order. In purchasing stocks, there are two main ways to do it.

1. **Utilizing a brokerage**

   This is the most common method to buying stocks. Brokerages generally come in two types. Full-service ones are more expensive but they will supposedly offer you expert inputs regarding stocks trading and manage your account. However, if you are confident with your knowledge in stocks trading, you can go for discount brokerages that are significantly much cheaper compared to full-service ones, the former of which you should note will only provide you little personal attention.

   With the advent of the Internet, there are many brokers out there that you can seek to help you out. Online discount brokers are available to assist you in investing in the stock market.

In choosing your broker, though, you need to ensure that even at this early step, you are choosing the right one so your success in making money out of stocks trading will be further cemented. Look for those with a stockbroker license. You should also take into consideration the quality of the customer service provided by any potential brokers. Do some research online and watch out for any reviews or ratings that could tell you any information about the broker. More importantly, find out if you can afford that commission rate of your broker. Choose those who can give you high quality service at a reasonable commission rate. And do not settle for those with extremely low commissions because they may turn out to be completely inexperienced and incompetent. Moreover, make it a point to know if your prospective broker possesses the necessary trading tools that can abet you in stocks trading such as market news, trading charts, latest stock quotes, etc.

2. Through DRIPs & DIPs

DRIPs or dividend reinvestment plans and DIPs or direct investment plans are plans that companies offer to shareholders. These plans allow stockholders to buy stocks directly from the company. As these plans are at a minimal cost, they are good ways to invest small amounts of money regularly.

Chapter 4   Trading the Right Stocks

Now that you know how to trade stocks, let us go over the characteristics of the stocks that you should purchase and sell to make money. This matter is very important since intimately knowing your stocks will give you an idea if you are going to be able to benefit from it.

How many shares to buy

How much stock should you buy to generate money? What is the safe size of your order to ensure that you will not lose money? You need to think on these questions very carefully as they will spell out your success.

The size of your order refers to the number of shares that you want to trade. And you need to know that most service charge you for every transaction and not per size of your order. This means that when you purchase 100 shares of Company A at one dollar per share, it would not just cost you $100. You will also be charged by your purchase order. Let us say that every purchase order costs $10. You will then have to pay a total amount of $110. So, if you will not purchase your shares in one go, it will cost you more. Having ten separate purchases of 10 stocks of Company A will cost you $200 in total.

Another thing that you have to take into consideration in buying stocks are your two options when it comes to purchasing them.

1. Round lots

    Buying stocks in round lots is akin to purchasing beer. Yes, people are free to buy beer individually if they want but there are also six-packs that most people actually prefer because not only are they more convenient to buy, they are also cheaper. A round lot is like a six-pack except for the fact that round lots do not come in the form of six shares. Usually, round lots are in groups of one hundred.

    Traders, when they avail of shares in round lots, pay lesser service charges and avail of the advantage of lower prices per share.

    For your information, there are also those that are traded in round lots of ten and are known as cabinet stocks. But, cabinet stocks are traded in groups of ten because of their exorbitant prices. Their prices can be in the tens of thousands of dollars and can come off as very expensive to average investors. Cabinet stocks are usually traded among wealthy institutions and individuals.

2. Odd lots

    Unlike round lots, odd lots is trading stocks that are fewer than a hundred shares or in the case of cabinet stocks, less than 10. With odd lots, price per share is higher but there are advantages to it that entice a significant amount of investors. For one, odd lots make it possible for you to purchase the exact number of stocks that you want. If you fancy buying 33 shares or 99, you do not have to worry about what you will do with the rest as in round lot purchases. Moreover, there is also the benefit of being able to buy by amount instead of by share. Case in point, you wish to buy $200 worth of stock from Company B. With their stock at $20 per share, by buying in an odd lot, you can purchase 10 shares of Company B.

How to buy shares

The next step after figuring out how much stocks to buy and if you want them in either round or odd lots is pinpointing how to order your stock. Orders pertain to instructions that you give your broker to inform him under what situation the stocks that you want should be bought or sold.

In this section, I am going to go over the points that you need to consider when it comes to your orders.

Two of the most common types of order is market order and limit order, the former of which refers to an order to trade stock at its best available price. In general, market orders are executed immediately at the risk of the price not being guaranteed. You need to remember, if you ever give out a market order, that the last-traded price of the stock is not necessarily the same price at which your market order will be executed. Especially in fast-moving markets, there will be deviations from the last-traded price to the price of your market order.

For example, if you put a market order to buy 10 shares of Company A when the best offer price was $5 per share, your order may be executed at a higher price if other orders from other investors are executed first.

With limit orders, an order to buy or sell a specific stock is at a set price. This means that a buy limit order may only be executed at the price it is limited to or lower and a sell limit order may only be executed at the price it is limited to or higher. The thing about limit order is there is not guarantee that it will be executed as it can only be fulfilled if the market price of the stock reaches its limit price. For example, if you want to buy shares of Company A's stock for no more than $5, you could put a limit order for $5. The order to buy the stock will only be fulfilled if its price is $5 or lower.

There are also other kinds of order such as day orders. This type of order is actually what's seen in majority of transactions. For example, if you instruct your broker to purchase 50 shares of Company C's stocks today and makes it clear that buying the stocks tomorrow is not feasible, the instruction is called day order. It is understandable why many transactions are day orders since performing trades in the future could be risky as they will be subjected to price fluctuations and market volatility. Nonetheless, you actually still have the option of keeping your order longer than a day.

Picking which stocks

Now that you have achieved a better understanding of stocks in general and what you need to consider in terms of amount and the way you order, let us proceed to discussing which stocks will be your best bet to making money easily.

First, before you can pinpoint what type of stocks would be your new best friend, you need to figure out what you are working hard for.

One of the biggest mistake that someone could commit when it comes to making money is failing to set a goal. Setting objectives makes everything easier because that way, you will know how far you will have to go, which methods would be most effective, and what will be your reward at the end of the road. For some people, they want to make money easy and fast to be able to purchase large-scale items like a house or a vehicle. How about you? What do you need your money for? Whether it is for your children's college fund or so you could just secure your financial status, it matters not as long as you have a vision in mind. However, you must take note that your goal must be concrete and achievable.

Once you have your objective already in mind, you can go over several of the different types of stock that could contribute to the fruition of your goal.

1. Income stock

   For investors who wished to have a regular supplemental income out of their investments, income stock could be your trusted companion. And this type of stock is not just for those who are looking for another source of income as it could also be the option for people who got a windfall of cash that they do not want to spend all at once. Income stocks are particularly designed to produce investments through dividend payments on a regular basis.

2. Growth stock

   With two categories namely conservative and aggressive stocks, growth stock is most popular among those who wants to invest. Individuals who are interested in education savings and retirement plans, among others, buy growth stocks.

   Valued because of their potential, growth stocks are purchased by individuals who believe that their value will go up instead of buying them for the objective of receiving regular dividend payments. If you purchase this kind of stock, you can make money out of it by selling the stock, once it has reached its potential price, for more than you bought it for.

Buying growth stocks is an excellent step to consider especially if you are still a beginner in stocks trading.

3. Speculative stock

If you consider yourself brave and adventurous, speculative stock could be your cup of tea.

Purchased for short-term gain, speculative stocks are considered precarious especially for new investors since they honestly have not honed yet the ability to pick a stock that will increase considerably in value in a short amount of time. Even experienced investors fail when they trade speculative stocks so make sure, in case you are interested in this kind of stock, that you are ready for whatever may happen.

Chapter 5   Trading Stocks Smartly

Along with making sure that you are knowledgeable enough about the mechanics of stocks trading, buying stocks smartly is a very good path to take to making good money.

So, what is the smart way to buy stocks? Simply enough, the answer is to have information. Having information about the company, for one, lets you know if you are getting your hands on stocks with good value. Without any inkling about the stocks that you are going to buy, any other strategy is useless.

There are many platforms where you can get the facts about companies that can help you in sizing up prospects for their stocks. A good source of these facts would be the company's annual report, which will reveal basic information about the company including an audited financial data. Annual reports are usually available from brokers and the investor relations office associated with the company.

Another source of information would be the form 10-K that contains in-depth financial data that companies file yearly as per request of the Securities and Exchange Commission. Form 10-K details two-year's worth of financial balance sheets and a 5-year history of data such as dividends, profits, and stock prices.

There are also analysts' reports available from brokers, which contain commentaries from brokerage firms. These reports hold analysts' suggestions when it comes to buy, selling, and holding a certain company's stocks.

When you already have the right information in your hands, it is time to apply what you have known in choosing the stocks that will prove healthy. To succeed in the stock market and get that money that you want, the efficient way of doing it would be to trade stocks with growth and value. In analyzing whether a stock would be profitable for you, you need to take note of the tests and indicators that I will present next in this section. Take note that stocks that meet the indicators and tests that will be presented shortly will be few. So what you should be in the lookout for are stocks that most of the tests. These stocks should then be included in the core of your portfolio.

1. Price-earnings ratio

The key here is to look for companies whose price-earnings ratio are lower than that of other companies.

P/E ratio is considered an intensely vital thing to know about stock and refers to the stock's current price divided by the company's earnings per stock. For example, if Company D's stock sells at $100 per share and the company gained $10 per share during the previous twelve months, the stock has a price-earnings ratio of 10. P/E ratio guides you on how much money traders are willing to pay for every dollar of a company's earnings. P/E ratios, because of its importance, are usually listed in newspapers alongside the stock's price.

When you are comparing P/E ratios, you need to do it among similar companies. If the stock you are on the lookout for is in the telecommunications industry, compare it to companies coming from the same industry.

2. Earnings per share

Earnings per share or EPS is the amount of dividends paid per share of stock owned by the company.

Look for companies that display a pattern of profit growth and the tendency of reinvesting a considerable portion of the earnings for the growth of the business.

3. Current/dividend yield

The current or dividend yield is the company's dividend represented as a percentage of the share price. So, if a share of stock is selling for $100 and the company pays $4 annually in dividends, the yield is 4%. As a stockholder, dividends does not just interest you because of it being a source of income but also since it serves as an effective indicator of a company's strength. If the company's history reveals rising dividends, this indicates that it is healthy and it manages to produce payouts at any given period.

4. Current and debt ratios

This ratio tells you how much debt or leverage the company has compared to its equity (total amount of assets). For example, if Company A has a total of $2 billion in shareholder's equity and $500 million in debt, the debt-equity ratio is 0.25 or 25%. The rule is the lower the ratio, the better. It would also be ideal if you consider buying stocks from companies that have debts that are no more than 35% of its equity.

Looking for the indicators that I have discussed above will go a long way in helping you to make the most money from your ventures. While you would need to face numbers and equations, the effort of understanding such figures will be worth it once you have attained your goal at the end of the day. But aside from the tests that your desired stocks would need to go through, there are also other scenarios that could help you determine the value of stocks and figure out if buying them would be smart.

For one, if the company whose stocks you are intending to buy is a leader in the industry it is in, it certainly gives you some sort of guarantee as to its profitability. As an industry leader, your company has an influence on the pricing of the products and because of its presence in the market, there is a high probability that products will be patronized.

Moreover, if the company's industry is on the rise, it could also be an indicator that the stock is good. Between a declining industry and a rising one, it does not take a brain which of the two you would more likely to succeed in. Young and growing industries hold a potential that could yield amazing profits. Just remember that there are also risks that come hand in hand with this potential.

Chapter 6   Commonly Made Mistakes and How to Avoid Them

With everything that you have learned so far, I hope you were able to pick up on what you need to do to make easy money from trading stocks. But before you go and enter fully the world of stocks and trading them, you still need to be aware of the mistakes that people usually commit so you could veer away from them.

1. Overtrading

Keep your capital in mind. Your capital is in the form of money and it is very valuable since its existence makes it possible for you to trade. If you make the mistake of overtrading, you increase your risk or losing. Particularly during poor market conditions, monitor how much you are trading.

2. Investing before you are ready

Investing and getting into any kind of business before you are financially ready will be disadvantageous for you. Yes, the primary reason why you might have started trading stocks is a lack in your funds but that deficiency is the leading reason why you will not be able to get out alive of this field. Sufficient funds is needed so you will be able to buy and sell shares. Without money, you would not be able to engage in transactions.

3. Avoiding diversification

One of the common mistakes traders do is failing to diversify their portfolio by sticking to one industry. To reduce risk, you should buy and sell stocks from different sectors. You can even go beyond the stock market. This way, your money is spread amongst various types of investments. If in case one sector experiences major problems, you can breathe easy with the thought that you still have a stake on other sectors out there.

4. Acting on tips

Be careful about tips that you get from your friends and acquaintances. Especially when they are compelling, investors make the mistake of giving in and following these tips. Before you place orders, make sure that you know something about the stocks that your friends are recommending.

5. Getting impatient

In every aspect of life, patience is needed to see favorable results at the end of the day. When nothing happens right away to your stocks, do not be miserable. For some stocks, it is easy to make money but it can probably take time depending on the industry that you are in.

Conclusion

Thank you again for downloading this book!

Trading stocks, for those who are beginners at it, can be a daunting task. It involves the use of money and there are risks that one should take in order to see the results that you are looking for.

Just remember that in order to get the most out of trading stocks, keep yourself informed on stock market news to know when you should pounce. Avail yourself of market updates from various sources such as The Wall Street Journal.

It is also recommended that you avoid spending all of your money by purchasing stocks in one go. Put your money in at various times and trade in different industries.

Moreover, when it comes to any trading strategies that you may learn to employ in the future, stick to what you understand. Do not jeopardize your money by utilizing a trading strategy that you know nothing about as this simply screams trouble.

Set a goal for yourself. Objectives are very important to keep you in line and motivate you to strive hard to meet them. Remember, your goals can also determine which type of stock would be most appropriate for you so as early as now, think about what you want to do with the money that you are going to earn from trading stocks.

Trading stocks is a highly logical transaction. Do not let your emotions take over and affect your decision-making. Do not buy and sell stocks just because you feel like it because you will definitely get emotional, at the end of the day, when it fails. Stick to your plan and remain faithful to your research. If you have determined a certain company to have good stocks, trust in the information that you have garnered.

Most importantly, realize that trading stocks is another venture where you can win and lose. Arm yourself with the knowledge and skills to win at trading stocks but if there comes a time when you lose, do not be afraid of taking it. Understand why you failed in that certain transaction and learn from the experience.

Like all other endeavors out there, trading stocks is a learning experience. Learn how it could help you improve your life and enjoy the benefits that it could give you.

Finally, if you enjoyed this book, then I'd like to ask you for a favor, would you be kind enough to leave a review for this book on Amazon? It'd be greatly appreciated!

Thank you and good luck!

www.ingramcontent.com/pod-product-compliance
Lightning Source LLC
Chambersburg PA
CBHW070754180526
45168CB00004B/1614